Naked and Not Ashamed
Application Journal

We've Been Afraid to Reveal What God Longs to Heal

Bishop T.D. Jakes

Treasure House

An Imprint of

Destiny Image Publishers, Inc.®

P.O. Box 310

Shippensburg, PA 17257-0310

"For where your treasure is
there will your heart be also." Matthew 6:21

ISBN 1-56043-259-4

For Worldwide Distribution
Printed in the U.S.A.

Treasure House books are available through these fine distributors outside the United States:

Christian Growth, Inc.
Jalan Kilang-Timor, Singapore 0315

Vine Christian Centre
Mid Glamorgan, Wales, United Kingdom

Rhema Ministries Trading
Randburg, South Africa

Vision Resources
Ponsonby, Auckland, New Zealand

Salvation Book Centre
Petaling, Jaya, Malaysia

WA Buchanan Company
Geebung, Queensland, Australia

Successful Christian Living
Capetown, Rep. of South Africa

Word Alive
Niverville, Manitoba, Canada

Inside the U.S., call toll free to order:
1-800-722-6774

Contents

Suggested Uses for This Application Journal

How to Use This Application Journal

Introduction

Chapter 1   The Fear of the Father 1

Chapter 2   No Secrets in the Secret Place 4

Chapter 3   Superman Is Dead. 7

Chapter 4   The Power of Passion. 10

Chapter 5   Reaping the Rewards of Your Own Thoughts. 13

Chapter 6   The Cold Kiss of a Calloused Heart 16

Chapter 7   Survive the Crash of Relationships 19

Chapter 8   Help! My New Heart Is Living in an Old Body! 22

Chapter 9   No Additives: The Blood Alone. 25

Chapter 10   He Laid Aside His Garments 29

Chapter 11   Stripped for Prayer 33

Answer Key. 37

Suggested Uses
for This Application Journal

- Individual study
- Small groups
- Bible studies
- Cell groups or care groups
- Sunday school classes

How to Use This Application Journal

Group Sessions

As a group session leader, you can either teach a session and have your group, on their own time, read the assignment and work in the journal; or you can have the people read the assignment before you come together to work on the journal as a group. In a large group, it is suggested that, at the leader's discretion, discussion groups of four to five people be formed to make it easy for people to share within a reasonable structure and time period.

Individual Study

If you are studying alone, you can read a chapter and work in the journal—Bible and pen handy—all together. Whenever the journal asks you to discuss or share a thought with someone else, simply consider the question in your own heart and allow the Holy Spirit to dialogue with your spirit on each issue.

Introduction

To really learn a principle or truth, you need to see it, hear it, and feel it. Writing about it, discussing it, and meditating on it all help to get it down into your innermost being. Applying it to your life and working it out in everyday situations anchor that truth even more deeply. Teaching, or discipling, then completes the process.

This application journal has been carefully designed to help you capture and apply the life-changing truths found in the book, *Naked and Not Ashamed*, by Bishop T.D. Jakes. Because Bishop Jakes carefully ministers in a way that gently but persistently demands an individual response, this journal will ask more of you than simply making check marks. You will be asked to respond personally and honestly to some difficult issues—because God is determined to make you whole, strong, and anointed in His service!

Chapter 1

The Fear of the Father

1. No matter how ___Strong___ we are, there is always something that can cause the ___Heart___ to flutter and the pulse to ___Raise___ .

2. Fear is ___D___ . It can cause:
   a. paralysis of the brain
   b. our thoughts to become arthritic
   c. our memory to become sluggish
   d. all the above
   Describe some of the other "telltale signs" or ways that fear affects your physical body and mental state:
   _____
   _____

3. What does this phrase mean to you? "From the football field to the ski slope, fear has a visa or entrance that allows it to access the most discriminating crowd" (choose all that apply):
   a. Fear is primarily limited to financial and banking people at football stadiums and on ski slopes.
   b. Fear mostly hits discriminating people.
   c. Fear can go anywhere and strike anybody, no matter how rich or poor they are.
   d. Fear can hit me even when I am doing my favorite things or surrounded by my friends.

4. When Bishop Jakes described the "fear of the innocent" and talked about his childhood fears, I could personally identify with:
   a. the fear of a child walking into a dark basement
   b. the fear that every "mop and bucket" was becoming a sinister creature
   c. the feeling that my heart had turned into "an African tom-tom" that was being beaten by an insane musician
   d. being held hostage in a prison of icy anxiety by my fear
   e. the ghosts and goblins of my "youthful closet of fear"
   f. the fearful little child hiding within my adult body who "peeks out" like a cautious turtle in a sometimes frightening world
   Please explain each of the answers you chose above: _____
   _____
   _____

5. God understands the ___Hidden___ ___CHild___ within each of us. He understands the ___Child___ ___in___ ___US___ , and He speaks to (Choose all that apply):
   a. the fashionably dressed adult I've become
   b. the well-adjusted survivor in me
   c. somebody else. I can't relate to any of this because…
   d. the blanket-clutching, thumb-sucking infantile need in me
   e. the childhood issues of the aging heart

6. My parents also think I'm still a child, "hiding in the darkness of adulthood," and (choose all that apply):
   a. sometimes, I wish I could run home to them and feel safe again
   b. I resent it, because: _____
   c. they're right, especially when: _____
   _____.

7. "The Lord looks beyond our *facade* and sees the *trembling places* in our lives." *Facade* in this passage means:
   a. an old interior design technique
   b. a false face used to conceal something behind it
   c. a carnival building

Personal Application: Describe *facades* you have seen in others: _____
_____
_____
_____

Are there any *facades* in your own life? Please explain: _____
_____
_____
_____

8. *Trembling places* in the quote above refers to:
   a. fearful places in our hearts, or situations we fear
   b. old memories from childhood that bring up unpleasant emotions
   c. my failures, especially the ones that happen again and again
   d. unknown areas that make me want to shrink back from the future.

Personal Application: Please give examples for each answer you chose: _____
_____
_____
_____
_____
_____

9. When Bishop Jakes says we must trust God alone "to see the very worst in us, yet still think the very best of us," I:
   a. just can't believe God could really think good things about me—not after what I've done!
   b. didn't realize that God really does see "the very worst in us." All this time, I kept thinking my secrets were only known to me
   c. think it's too good to be true! If it's really true, then for the first time in my life I have nothing to hide from God
   d. wish somebody on earth would treat me the same way

NOTE: Please discuss your answers to this question with others, if possible, and listen to their comments about their choices.

10. When I hear someone say, "The love of a father," I think (choose all that apply):
    a. I wish I knew what it was like, but I never knew my father. I hope I can experience it in my lifetime
    b. of my own father, who loved me even when I made mistakes. Somehow I think of him when I think of God
    c. of my father, but I never connect him with love. The pain I feel when I think of Dad is so intense, I know something in me has to change before I can know God as "Father"
    d. I feel excited and free. I feel like I can do anything I dare to dream as long as God is with me

Personal Application: Discuss your answers with others, if possible. How do you feel when you hear the comments of someone who chose a different answer than you did? Talk about it with them before moving on to the next question. (If you are going through this application journal independently, carefully think about each of the answers and try to understand the implications they would have for someone learning to love his heavenly Father.)

11. When Jesus taught His disciples how to pray, the first thing He taught them was to:
    a. always kneel and properly fold their hands before bowing their heads
    b. climb into a closet together so their prayers would be private
    c. acknowledge the fatherhood of God

12. The basis of our relationship with God is:
    a. our church membership
    b. our physical bloodlines as traced back through our ancestors to Abraham and Adam
    c. our sonship through Jesus Christ, who grafts us into His divine family
    d. our good deeds and noble thoughts in this life

13. When Bishop Jakes says, "Knowing your father helps you understand your own _____ as a _____ or _____," I feel:
    a. happy and secure because I know my father, and I know how he feels about me
    b. sad and hopeless because I never knew my father. I can only believe that he didn't really think much of me, or he would have been there
    c. upset because I still don't want anything to do with my natural father. He left us, and I can't help but fear that God might leave me too

Personal Application: Please share your answer with someone else. If you chose answers b or c, look up Psalm 68:5 and James 1:27. Discuss with each other how these apply.

14. The Bible says we should _____ the Lord and _____ from evil (Prov. 3:7). The modern meaning of "fear" has connotations of _____, but that is not a _____ _____ for a child of God. The original Hebrew word for "fear" could be better translated as "_____."

15. We are not to live in "terror" of God because we are _____ in our _____ with Him. His _____ holds His judgment in balance.

16. God may not _____ of your conduct, but He still _____ you.

17. The Church has confused _____ with _____.

18. Which one of the above leads to deliverance and change? _____

19. Regardless of the atrocious behavior we discover when we work with the flawed material of human insufficiency, we must remember that the only antidote is:
    a. better government programs and more money to fund them
    b. to build more prisons and boost the police force
    c. to educate people out of their sin
    d. in the presence of the Lord

Chapter 2

No Secrets in the Secret Place

1. Most of us "tiptoe around in the presence of God" as if we could tiptoe softly enough not to _____
   a _____ who never _____ nor _____.

2. When Bishop Jakes writes, "I, for one, need a Father whose wrinkled up eyes can see beyond my broken places and know the longing of my heart," the phrase "wrinkled up eyes" refers to:
   a. a geriatric deity
   b. an infinitely wise and all-knowing God who looks beyond the "surface appearances" in our lives
   c. a God who is nearly blind

3. It is the nature of fallen man to:
   a. leave a bar and carefully avoid the open church door on the way home
   b. constantly play music or have the TV on to avoid being alone with their "thoughts"
   c. hide behind bushes and aprons of fig leaves when God comes near "the morning after" a sin
   d. all the above

4. When we hide from God, we lose ourselves. The only cure is to come out from _____
   _____ _____ and become _____ in the presence of the Lord.

5. Like Adam, whose sin led him to hide from God in fear, our fear can cause us to _____ to
   _____ our only Solution (God).

Personal Application: If applicable, pick the confession most appropriate for you and discuss it with someone else.
   a. Like a drug addict or alcoholic who fears going through life without the help of his addiction will hide his drugs and booze, I've hidden _____ from God and man.
   b. Like a child who is afraid to reveal the half-eaten cookie in his hand to his mother who is calling him to dinner, I'm afraid to show God what I was doing when He called me into His presence.
   c. Like the heart patient caught in a donut shop by his physician, I'm tempted to say to God, "Oh, I just came by to show these folks what to avoid so they won't be like me."
   d. Other: _____

6. Although many Christians are intimidated by God's holiness, we need to realize that we are accepted by God because we are _____ _____ and dressed because His Son, Jesus Christ, has _____ us in His _____ _____.

7. If you hide from God's perfect love, you will never be able to:
   a. _____ a _____ with your heavenly Father
   b. be comfortable enough to _____ in His _____
   c. be _____ by Him
   d. find healing for the _____ of life and for our _____ _____

Personal Application: What would your life be like without these things? _____
_____
_____

8. I know that the basis of any relationship must be trust, but (choose and discuss the answer of your choice):
   a. is there anyone I can share my secret thoughts with?
   b. is there someone I can trust enough to tell my inner failures and fears?
   c. is there anyone who won't be shocked by the secrets and hidden things I share?

Personal Application: Obviously Bishop Jakes was referring to God as our ultimate Friend and Counselor who already knows all things. However, what can we learn about the character of God that would apply to our friendships and relationships with one another? _____

_____

_____

_____

9. Once we realize that the Lord "knoweth the thoughts of man, that they are vanity" (Ps. 94:11), then all our attempts at _____ and _____ seem juvenile and _____. Why? _____

_____

10. We are balanced by our awareness of God's holiness, which would _____ _____, and of His love, which _____ and _____ us.

11. God is far too holy for me to _____ _____ about my humanity, yet He is far too loving for me to be _____ by my _____ _____.

12. "When I am properly understood, I don't always have to express and explain." To me, this means: _____

_____

13. You are called to live in a state of _____ - _____ _____ with the Lord because (choose all that apply):
   a. it is part of your eschatological theory
   b. it makes your religion more realistic and acceptable
   c. you need someone who is able to help you
   d. you need someone who is able to understand the issues of your heart

14. We are naked before God in the same sense that a man sprawls naked _____ _____ _____ _____ before a _____. Our exposed condition is a necessity of our relationship. How might this truth apply to your own life: _____

_____

_____

15. Our comfort lies in the conviction that the Great Physician possesses the wherewithal to (choose the best answer):
   a. supply us with a new car
   b. relieve the symptoms of our disease
   c. restore order in any area that may be in disarray
   d. keep us from feeling any pain

16. Purity in our lives comes when we allow God to "perpetually flush away the corrosion that threatens to block the abundant arterial flow of His grace and mercy toward us." This "corrosion" can be:
   a. the "cholesterol" of indigestible disobedience and reluctance to obey God
   b. the buildup of bitterness that clings to old wounds
   c. the fatty deposits of fear that block the arteries of God's supply from reaching our innermost parts
   d. the floating blood clots from unhealed wounds of the past that continually threaten us with aneurysms and spiritual paralysis from strokes

Personal Application: Please discuss the points in question 16 with another.

17. God is continually sending a deluge of His _____ _____ into the hearts of His chil-
    dren, but He can't _____ or _____ what we _____ in the _____
    _____ of our hearts and minds.

18. Bishop Jakes came to the understanding that the slate of sin had been _____ _____
    _____, but that his mind was being _____ from _____ _____
    _____. Does this apply to your life too? How? _____
    _____

19. There is a peace that comes from knowing you are God's child. It comes from knowing you are His—even
    when you feel like (pick the answer that best describes your feelings):
    a. everything you touch goes wrong
    b. your problems are so embarrassing and crude that you can't discuss them with anyone
    c. you are paralyzed with anger over your weaknesses and flaws because they continually arise to mess
        up your life
    d. you are not worthy or good enough for anyone's love, let alone God's love

20. You will never _____ God _____ if you live in the shadows, _____ with
    _____ sin.

21. Open relationships with other people can never be attained until you first _____
    _____ _____ and _____ _____ before God. If you cannot
    _____ Him, then all _____ is lost.

Chapter 3

Superman Is Dead

1. Where did the heroes go? We need someone who:
   a. is perfect, untarnished, and above all forms of temptation
   b. who would never experience the lowly challenges or failures we face every day
   c. has superhuman strength and stands out from the crowd with his or her bright costume
   d. has accomplished something to give us the courage to believe in the invisible and feel the intangible

2. Our healing will require more than impotent and irrelevant religious ideas; we need to:
   a. put on our best face and let the healing "come from within"
   b. buy season tickets to a psychotherapy clinic
   c. go to God and tell Him, "This is where I am hurting"

3. It takes _____ _____ to exemplify total honesty with God. When we discover our own _____, we become eligible to discover the all-_____ of God! What areas of limitation have you discovered in your life?_____
   _____
   _____

4. God knew who we were when He called us. He knew all about our sins, our fears, and our mistakes. If His intent is to establish believable heroes, are you a candidate?
   a. List two significant crises you have survived with God's help: _____
   _____
   _____
   b. List the most serious sin you have managed to overcome by God's grace: _____
   c. Who do you think needs a hero like you the most? (See the Answer Key for a hint.) _____
   _____
   _____

5. Describe the formula used to make our leaders die in the pulpit and suffer from an epidemic of stress: _____
   _____
   _____

6. Paul openly confessed his shortcomings, yet we continually _____ _____
   _____ _____ from his _____ _____ .

7. The "calling" Paul described in Philippians 3:13-14 was high, but it was answered by _____ men who could see God high and lifted up. In short, the _____ in the Bible were _____ _____, but they were _____. How does this make you feel?_____
   _____
   _____

8. a. Define what a "hero" is: _____
   _____

    b.   Who matches this description more than any other person who ever lived? _____

_____

    c.   Is there a way or an event in which you have matched this definition? Explain: _____

_____

9.   Sin stinks in the nostrils of God, but He saved us like Jesus saved Lazarus from the tomb. Thank God that
Jesus _____ _____ _____ _____ stop Him from

_____ _____ _____.

10. If you aspire to be a leader, be prepared to (complete each line):
    a.   expose yourself to the _____ and _____ of being raised up as a leader (see the
story of Joseph in Genesis 37–48)
    b.   be _____ by your peers
    c.   be _____ by your subordinates
    d.   _____ valiantly while receiving _____ from _____
    e.   receive _____ from friends
    f.   continue to _____ as if all were well through it all

11. There must be a _____ _____ of _____ lodged firmly in our minds that
dispels the despair of past failures. Describe in your own words how this could help you overcome failures in
your life: _____

_____

_____

_____

_____

12. "Believable heroes" must be resilient enough to survive tragedy and adversity because if they don't
_____, they can't _____ _____.

13. The thing that causes you to be different from others whose complacency you can't seem to share is:
    a.   your unique style and flare for chic fashion
    b.   your "go-getter" way of tackling life
    c.   your body shape, your upbringing, your financial position, and your church membership
    d.   your convictions

14. The valiant Bible heroes listed in Hebrews 11 were _____ that what God had _____
He was _____ _____ _____. Their lives are living proof that
"_____ always _____ in the _____ of their mind." What is your mind
full of right now? _____

_____

Are you sure you want to go in that direction? _____

15. To be a real success, we must be able to be strengthened through struggle. When we see that the believable
heroes of God have a "dent in their armor," we should:
    a.   carefully and loudly warn others about their fault
    b.   cover it up and pretend it doesn't exist
    c.   consider their entire life, and see that the dent in their armor doesn't affect their performance on the
battlefield
Please explain why each of these is true or false: _____

_____

_____

_____

_____

16. Jephthah, the "reject" who gathered other rejects together to form an Old Testament gang, actually built an "_____ of _____" that delivered his nation. It is God's design that causes us to _____ _____, even though it is painful. Have you ever felt misplaced because of rejection? Explain. Did it make you bitter or better? Explain: _____

    _____

    _____

17. The pain of rejection and misplacement causes us to:
    a. say, "Forget the whole thing, God; I want out"
    b. meekly back up and accept the fact that we're losers, and that "some things never change"
    c. strike back in anger and resentment
    d. achieve a level of consecration that is out of the reach of people who have never been rejected

18. God created "a _____ for the _____" and chose us for Himself. For this reason, is it possible that we have forsaken some of God's finest people because they were under attack? What is your opinion? _____

    _____

19. God is still in the "business" of _____ human _____! Perhaps the revival must start:
    a. in the trash cans of our churches
    b. in the dumpsters of ministries that have discarded what God regarded, and regarded what God has discarded
    c. in the trenches, the foxholes, and the hogpens of life
    d. all the above

20. No worship seminar is needed for:
    a. well-trained seminary and music school graduates
    b. long-standing members of the community choir
    c. members of "our" denomination
    d. someone whose tear-stained face has turned from humiliation to inspiration

Chapter 4

The Power of Passion

1. There is an underlying _____ beneath the _____ of the cross, which the writer of Hebrews addressed when he looked behind the _____ of the _____ and reported the _____ of the _____.

2. Jesus endured the pain and suffering of the cross:
    a. because He looked across the gulf of time and saw us serving Him today
    b. because it was the only way to pay our debt and redeem us
    c. because He loved us so much
    d. for the joy that was set before Him
    e. all the above

3. The _____ of fulfillment lies in this truth: There can be no _____ where there is _____ _____. The passion that causes us to achieve has to be strong enough to make us _____.

4. It is the force of your _____ _____ to _____ that gives you the force to break down the _____ between you and the thing you desire. Describe the "things" you desire, along with the wall separating you from them: _____
   _____
   _____

5. The "fuel" that enables us to withstand whatever life sends against us is:
    a. purely the power of positive thinking
    b. youthfulness
    c. money, influence, and education
    d. the God-implanted desire that inflames our hearts and is forever in our thoughts

6. _____ is the intense discomfort associated with _____ and _____.

7. God loves to use people who (choose all that apply):
    a. know how to please everybody
    b. avoid making waves; who know how to live well while risking little
    c. are accustomed to passion and acquisition—even if it was misdirected at one time or another
    d. who dare to desire with a burning passion, but who are open to His direction

Personal Application: Discuss and write down your comments about the truth or falsehood in each answer above.
_____
_____
_____

8. If you have great passion, then you should:
    a. probably kill it before it kills you!
    b. present it as a tool of satan to destroy you

    c. control it, not kill it; God created you to be zesty and alive

    d. put your passion in a religious receptacle to make it respectable

9. When we avoid the pain and suffering created by our passions, we (choose all that apply):
    a. wisely choose the path of least resistance, like nature
    b. may become like zombies, trapped in an intermediate, lukewarm, mediocre state of existence
    c. are just "going through the motions" of living
    d. we may become corpses who aren't quite dead

    Explain your answer: _____
    _____
    _____
    _____

10. Assuming you want to "make a difference," if you run into some obstacle or some cross, you should:
    a. adjust your expectations
    b. keep smiling
    c. throw in the towel and quit
    d. breathe deeply and know there will never be another moment in your life like this one

11. It is _____ you _____ that expresses how _____ you _____.
    What have you desired? What have you endured? Explain:_____
    _____
    _____

12. What could *not* be stripped away from Jesus when He was nailed to the cross at Calvary?
    a. His disciples and friends
    b. His clothes and ministry
    c. His passion

13. The love of Jesus Christ for us is _____ in His _____, but it is _____ in _____ _____ .

14. Where there is no passion, there simply _____ _____ _____. If we exist without passion:
    a. we'll live longer
    b. we'll live happier
    c. we'll slump into a state of stagnation
    d. we'll never achieve the purpose of God in our lives
    e. c and d

15. The enemy is trying to steal something from you! It is (more than one may apply):
    a. not visible
    b. stolen quickly and with great violence
    c. depleted slowly like air escaping silently from a tire
    d. something that can be stolen from you without detection

16. This treasure is the _____ of the _____ that is locked in the recesses of your _____. Out of the _____ flow the _____ of _____.

17. You can't spend the rest of your life trying to protect yourself from the struggles of life because:
    a. you're too busy making money and staying on top of things
    b. they are unavoidable
    c. if you become intimidated, you will live your life in an emotional incubator—insulated but isolated
    d. b and c

18. We must no longer _____ on what can be _____. We must closely monitor:
    a. what we go through
    b. the pain we are strongly resisting
    c. the loss of passion

Personal Application: Please comment briefly on the value of each answer: _____
_____
_____

19. We who are on the _____ of _____ are always kept in a _____ state of
    _____! What does this mean to you? _____
    _____

20. What a joy to know that _____ can be _____ by _____ and still not lose
    its value! What does this say to you? _____
    _____

21. What controls the direction of our lives?
    a. the supreme force of circumstance
    b. our moods and emotional states
    c. our bosses, kings, and spouses
    d. "what we do with what we feel"

22. God knows there is no cure for *past pain* like _____ _____. As the desire and
    _____ to _____ comes creeping back into your life, come out of hiding and show
    yourself "_____ and not _____."

Chapter 5

Reaping the Rewards of Your Own Thoughts

1. We often resist loneliness by filling up our lives with _____ and with people who mean us _____ _____ at all. In contrast, God speaks to us in our "aloneness" and becomes our _____ _____—always seeking out what is _____ for us.

2. The eyes of Bishop Jakes' grandmother revealed _____ buried deep beneath the ashes of her experience. She would "flee into the _____ of her own _____." Her silence was the mark of someone who has learned _____ _____ _____ _____.

3. The _____ eyes of the wise can make our _____ and _____ seem like the foolish ranting of a _____ mind. Has this ever happened to you? Explain. _____
   _____

4. God may speak through the eyes of an aged believer, telling you to _____ and _____
   _____. This depth of wisdom only comes from years spent alone, warming yourself at the _____ of your _____ _____ in communion with God.

5. We need to allow God to heal our thoughts because they are often the product of (pick the choice that best describes you, and discuss it among your group):
   a. damaged emotions
   b. traumatic events
   c. vicious opinions forced upon you by domineering people

6. One of your greatest challenges as a Christian is to resist the temptation to allow what happened _____
   _____ _____ to determine who you are today. We must declare: "I am not what _____ _____. I _____ what happened. I _____ what happened, but I am _____ _____ _____ yesterday!"

Personal Application: Think of your most painful memory or hurt and *boldly declare these things* about it in the name of Jesus Christ!

7. You must remember that you don't have to watch the "movie" in your mind if you are not enjoying what is being played. That's right—hit the _____ _____ over your thoughts! Choose carefully what you meditate on because:
   a. you will ultimately become whatever it is you meditate upon
   b. the enemy starts every assault on your morality through a thought, not an act
   c. a thought is a seed that, if not aborted, will always produce offspring somewhere in your life
   d. all the above

8. The thoughts or seeds of satan only become "yours" when you allow them to _____
    _____ and _____ _____! An evil thought will rearrange your
    _____, your _____, and your _____ (that is a very powerful
    house guest).

9. Thoughts are:
    a. wisps of wind that have no substance and no power to hurt
    b. empty and vain imaginings of men that should be discarded
    c. previews of coming attractions; something to be acted on when savored long enough

10. None of us have fully conquered the battle of the mind. It is a _____ _____ that can
    easily become a secret place for contamination, lust, and God only knows what else! If everything that comes
    to your mind were played on a television screen before the church, it would resemble:
    a. the steamiest of daytime soap operas, with my fellow members in supporting roles around the star—me
    b. a twisted film with a theme of jealous intrigue, cherished revenge, and cruel murder
    c. a bitter tale of loves lost, love scorned, and endless loneliness and disappointment
    d. it is too embarrassing to even discuss

Personal Application: This question is *too personal* for most of us to discuss with any but our closest friends and
counselors, but it is profitable for honest reflection and assessment of our own character. No matter how unkept
our minds are, we can control our thoughts and allow Jesus Christ to renew our minds daily.

11. God loves you so much that He stays in the house you haven't fully cleaned. Match the appropriate parts
    below:
    a.   He hates   d. the thoughts
    b.   He despises   e. the thinker
    c.   He loves   f. the acts
    Why is it important to distinguish between these three things? _____
    _____
    _____

12. The mind is the "_____" of the spirit man. It:
    a. is a great restaurant featuring Mexican-style food
    b. holds and nurtures the seeds it has been impregnated with until their time of delivery
    c. should be surgically removed for our own good so we won't be contaminated

13. Most people who are unsuccessful in their lives do not lack talent. However, there seems to be (more than one
    may apply):
    a. genetic difficulties evident in most of them
    b. shackles of a poor environment, ethnicity, or upbringing that will forever hold them back
    c. some little thought they entertain that affects their tenacity or their commitment to excellence
    d. some dwarfed self-image or over-inflated ego that preempts them from reaching their aspirations

Personal Application: Why are some of the answers above true and some false? _____
_____
_____

14. Christ has a balanced mind. That means He:
    a. is uncomfortable with His exaltation
    b. carefully followed the controversial opinions of men to determine who He "thought" He was; His inner
        perception was flexible and variable so He would not offend anyone
    c. wrestled with arrogance, unsure of His reputation and earthly identity
    d. was the exact opposite of each answer given above, and that we should follow His lead and be free
        of the need to impress other people

15. God is constantly _____ lethal _____ that hinder us from grasping the many-faceted callings and giftings _____ beneath the _____ of our _____.

Personal Application: Carefully consider the meaning of the missing words. What comes to mind about your life as you ponder this statement and apply it to your personal life?_____
_____

16. We need to renew our minds daily in God's presence because:
    a. smarter is better
    b. we need to stuff our minds so full of "memorized Scripture" that there isn't room or time for anything else to catch us
    c. as we hear the thoughts of God, His thinking becomes increasingly contagious

17. The soft words of God _____ _____ the wrath of our _____ _____, and His words become _____ of _____ falling like soft rain on a tin roof, giving rest and peace.

18. There is a strong tie between _____ and _____. As Christians, we have discovered that there is _____ in our _____, and we have been taught to speak _____; however:
    a. even God works out of the reservoir of His own thoughts
    b. we were thinking one thing while the mouth was confessing something else
    c. our thoughts must align with our confession—otherwise, the house is divided against itself
    d. all the above

19. Your life will ultimately take on the direction of your thinking. Many weaknesses, such as procrastination and laziness, are (more than one may apply):
    a. impossible to shake without counseling and professional help
    b. simply the material you were given to work with at birth
    c. just draperies that cover up poor self-esteem and a lack of motivation
    d. often symptoms of the subconscious avoiding the risk of failure

20. Like Mephibosheth in Second Samuel 9, you may think of yourself as a dead dog, so you lay on the floor like one. *What word is God saying to you?*
    a. You have been on the floor long enough!
    b. It's time for a resurrection, and it is going to start in your mind.
    c. If you're afraid of losing God's blessing because you're unworthy—forget it! You're worthy because Jesus says you're worthy.
    d. Just because you've been treated like a dog doesn't make you one!

Personal Application: Mark the answer or answers that most apply to your life and explain them: _____
_____
_____

21. Hold on to your _____ of _____. If you can _____ _____ _____ _____ when men are trying to command a drought in your life, then God will mightily sustain you!

Chapter 6

The Cold Kiss of a Calloused Heart

1. The reason one relationship becomes more valuable than others is:
   a. we get more out of the relationship; the person can do more for us than other people
   b. because some people agree with us more than others and go along with what we want
   c. that the relationship has the ability to survive circumstances and endure realignments when it is tested by some threatening force

2. Having too many companions creates _____, absorbs _____, and cheapens _____. The object is _____, not _____.

3. God sees every imperfection we have and:
   a. He is determined to clean us up before we are allowed to fellowship with Him
   b. He regrets sparing Noah and his family from the Great Flood
   c. He says, "Somehow I didn't realize they'd gotten so bad!"
   d. He still maintains His commitment to "love the unlovely." He knows us, yet He understands and loves us anyway!

4. A true friend should desire to:
   a. help you meet the "right" person—even if it isn't your current spouse
   b. help you take care of "Number One" and order all your life priorities that way
   c. always find out what you want and agree with it—that's what friends do
   d. see you prosper in your marriage, in your finances, and in your health and spirituality

Personal Application: Please explain why you selected your answer: _____
_____
_____

5. The distress of betrayal in a relationship:
   a. can become a wall that insulates us
   b. isolates us from those around us
   c. is part of the risk of love
   d. can make you fear the bitter taste of rejection even more
   e. all the above

Personal Application: Please describe these experiences as they apply to your life: _____
_____
_____

6. The closeness of a covenant relationship is (more than one may apply):
   a. purely an Old Testament thing; nobody does that kind of thing anymore
   b. the wealth that causes street people to smile in the rain and laugh in the snow
   c. often seen among people whose only flame is the friendship of someone who relates to the plight of daily living
   d. something many wealthy people long to experience

Personal Application: Do you feel you have experienced this kind of rich covenant relationship? Please explain:

_____

_____

_____

7. Many people who are surrounded by crowds of co-workers, friends, and family members every day are still alone. They are:
    a. disenchanted with life
    b. professional actors on the stage of life
    c. unwilling to let anyone get too close
    d. afraid to risk the pain of a disappointed heart
    e. a picture of the way I feel

Personal Application: Please comment on each of the answers you selected above or discuss them with others:

_____

_____

_____

_____

8. God can give _____ out of _____. It was _____ ministry that brought Christ to the cross! Looking through the eyes of destiny, we can know that _____ is too _____ to have His plans _____ by the petty acts of men. Otherwise, constant _____ would _____ many of us from _____ possible _____ and covenant _____.

9. God doesn't intend for every _____ to _____. Why? _____

    _____

10. Since we serve the God "who _____ _____," the art to surviving painful moments is:
    a. to become a master of illusion and a skilled escape artist
    b. found in a bottle, a syringe, or a refrigerator
    c. to become a Bible scholar and philosopher
    d. living in the zone where we respond to God with a yes, whether the door is open or closed

11. If God allows a relationship to continue, and some _____, _____ _____ come from it, you must realize:
    a. you deserve it
    b. it's your fault because you got yourself into the mess
    c. God will only allow what ultimately works for your good

Personal Application: Which of these statements have you entertained in your experiences? Describe the situations, and what you think now: _____

_____

_____

_____

12. The unique thing about God's parenting is that He sometimes _____ a _____ to bring about a _____. If you don't understand the _____ of God, then all is lost.

13. We need a deep knowledge that:
    a. can only be attained through work toward an advanced college degree
    b. our destiny consists only of our choices, our genes, and our environment
    c. God is in control and He is able to reverse the adverse

Personal Application: Please comment on *each* of those answers: _____
_____
_____

14. Even in the most harmonious of relationships there are _____ and _____. It is important to realize that:
    a. nobody is as important as you are
    b. if you are going to succeed, it's up to you and nobody else
    c. God allows different people to come into your life to accomplish His purposes

15. Implied friendship describes my relationship with those who weren't consciously or obviously trying to help me, although they did. Since my ultimate goal is to please Christ Jesus, I must:
    a. dump these losers and purge my flock of friends
    b. run every friend through a "litmus test" of all-out commitment to "me"
    c. widen my definition of friendship to include the betrayer if his betrayal ushered me into the next step of God's plan for my life

16. Have you come to realize that there are some who are actually _____ in your blessing, although they never really _____ or _____ you as a person? Describe these friends from the "_____ _____" of your life: _____
_____
_____

17. No one helped Jesus reach His goal like:
    a. Peter, James, and John
    b. John the Baptist
    c. Mary, His mother, and the women who accompanied His party
    d. Judas

18. When you encounter a Judas in your life, remember that it is his or her _____ that carry out the _____ of _____ in your life! Your mysterious _____ of _____ and _____ may actually become the _____ for _____ in your life!

19. You must learn how to accept even the relationships that seem to be _____ or _____ because God, your Ultimate Friend (choose all that apply):
    a. will reject and desert you if you don't
    b. sometimes manipulates the actions of your enemies to cause them to work as friends
    c. can bless you through the worst of relationships
    d. knows how to make adversity feed destiny into your life

20. The real challenge is to sit at the table with a betraying Judas on one side and a loving John on the other, and to (choose all that apply):
    a. shoot one as many times as possible without harming the other
    b. genuinely enjoy the meal without having too much heartburn
    c. treat one no differently from the other, even though we are distinctly aware of each one's identity and agenda
    d. allow the sufferings of success to give us direction and build character in us

Personal Application: Please comment on each answer you selected as it applies to your own life: _____
_____
_____

21. "Betrayal is only sweetened when it is _____ _____ _____. *Live on, my friend, live on!*"

Chapter 7

Survive the Crash of Relationships

1. Our deep-seated need to _____ _____ is part of our superior _____ ability. It separates us from lower forms of life that tend to _____ _____ as they come.

2. We are sometimes disillusioned when we find out how easily people will leave us. Generally they leave us when:
    a. we run out of money
    b. we think that we need them
    c. we move from the successful stage to the struggling stage
    d. we are more aspiring than accomplished

3. God is determined to _____ us of our strong tendency to be _____ on others, thereby teaching us _____-_____ and _____-_____.

4. Emotional pain is to the spirit what _____ _____ is to the body. It warns us that we have an area that needs _____ or _____.

5. In spite of the pain and distaste of adversity, it is impossible not to notice:
    a. how good it was back in Egypt, before the desert, the manna, and the pillar of fire by night
    b. how pleased and smug our enemies seem to be about our situation
    c. that each adverse event leaves sweet nectar behind that, in turn, can produce its own rich honey in our character

Personal Application: What have you noticed during your times of distress and adversity? Describe your observations: _____
_____
_____
_____
_____

6. We can only benefit from _____ _____. The great tragedy is that most of us _____ our _____ active. We must allow the process of healing to:
    a. dump all our bitterness out on the "table" for everyone to see
    b. hide our pain and guilt from us
    c. take us far beyond bitterness into a resolution that releases us from the prison and sets us free

7. God's healing process makes us free to taste life again. Without it:
    a. we never want to trust again
    b. we want to be safe from life's threatening grasp, even if we are so detached from life that we lose consciousness of people, places, dates, and events
    c. we always talk about the past because we stopped living years ago at the time of our wounding
    d. we allow the past to steal the present right out of our hand
    e. all the above

Personal Application: Have you experienced any of these situations? Please explain: _____
_____
_____

8. It is time to celebrate—no matter what you have suffered or feared, you are alive! The choice is yours. You may:
    a. step into the present, realize you are alive, and celebrate!
    b. subject all your friends to another sad history class
    c. incessantly rage and blubber about that which no one can change
    d. jump start your heart and step back into the presence of a real experience far from the dank, dark valley of regret and remorse
    e. a and d
    f. b and c

9. The greatest of all depressions comes when we live and gather our successes just to prove something:
    a. to someone who isn't even looking
    b. done by us but not for us
    c. done in the name of a person, place, or thing that has moved on, leaving us in a time warp, wondering why we are not fulfilled
    d. for someone who will never appreciate what he or she can't detect
    e. all the above

Personal Application: Have you experienced any of these? Explain: _____
_____
_____

10. Your blessing has not been and never will be:
     a. available for you in "this life"
     b. something you can count on because you are just a sinner
     c. predicated upon the action of another

11. It is in the absence of human assistance that we can (more than one may apply):
     a. test the effectiveness of government programs
     b. test the limits of our resourcefulness
     c. experience the magnitude of the favor of God
     d. experience the birth of inner resilience, adapt, and see our survival instincts peak

12. We will never be selected by God for great things until:
     a. we have graduated from Bible school
     b. we can gather all the votes from the nominating committee and satisfy the personal tastes of every board member
     c. we have been through some degree of rejection, like David, Joseph, Moses, and Jesus Christ

13. If you want to be tenacious, you must be able to walk in the light of _____ _____ rather than dwell in the darkness of _____ _____. These critics are just a part of God's purpose in your life.

Personal Application: Have you been confronted by this kind of choice? Please describe it: _____
_____
_____

14. Focus is _____ in ministry. You will never be able to minister to the Lord if:
     a. your attention is distracted by the constant thirst of other people
     b. you are always trying to win people over
     c. you make idols out of other people and their opinions instead of focusing on God's opinions
     d. all the above

15. The Lord _____ what the enemy does and makes it _____ His _____ in your life. In the hands of God, even our most _____ _____ become marvelous in our eyes!

Personal Application: How many times have "evil" things happened in your life that you later realized were necessary? Describe them: _____

_____

_____

16. Rejection is only marvelous in:
    a. situations where promotion follows
    b. Heaven, where we feel no pain
    c. the eyes of someone whose heart has wholly trusted in the Lord, believing He is directing his or her steps and that He has the grace to correct it

17. Faith is not needed just to _____ problems; it is also needed to _____ problems that seem _____. It has the power to make the _____ _____ look good!

18. In the same way that a car crash causes injury, a crashing relationship:
    a. affects everyone associated with it
    b. has a varying effect, depending on the relationship
    c. can injure, but we don't have to die in the crashes and collisions of life; rather we must learn to live life with a spiritual and emotional seat belt in place
    d. all the above

19. The "seat belt" that stops you from going through the roof when you are rejected is:
    a. your reputation and credentials
    b. your positive appearance, sharp wardrobe, and past track record
    c. your inner assurance that God is in control, and that what He has determined no one can disallow!

Personal Application: Discuss the truth or falsehood of each of these answers: _____

_____

_____

_____

20. If God said He was going to _____ _____, then _____ the _____ and believe a God who _____ _____. The rubbish can be cleared and the _____ can be healed.

21. No matter how painful, devastated, or disappointed you may feel, just remember:
    a. you're still here; the smoke has cleared and you're still standing
    b. you are too important to the purpose of God to be destroyed by a situation that is only meant to give you character and direction
    c. God will use the cornerstone developed through rejections and failed relationships to perfect what He has prepared!
    d. that *all these* apply to *you*

Personal Application: If you're alive, you probably have scars on your "hide." They are more than monuments to your injury; they are proof that you *survived the crash*! Describe here one or more of the events or situations God has brought you through: _____

_____

_____

Chapter 8

Help! My New Heart Is Living in an Old Body!

1. You are moving onward in gradual transition from _____ _____ to _____ _____. Your goal is to eventually focus all _____ _____.

2. Many young (and old) Christians:
   a. have tried to become what they think all other Christians are
   b. secretly suffer from low self-esteem
   c. think the Christians around them have mastered a level of holiness that seems to evade them
   d. deeply admire those virtuous "faith heroes" with flowery testimonies
   e. earnestly pray, "Lord, make me better!"
   f. all the above, at one time or another

3. Bishop Jakes said his *motivation* changed once he realized that God knew him and loved him as he was. Before then, he thought:
   a. if you do good, then God _____ you
   b. if you don't, then God _____ love you
   c. it was like a _____ _____ ride
   d. all the above

4. Bishop Jakes said he looked at how good his friends seemed to be, and he:
   a. made new friends who lived more on his level
   b. gave up trying to become an "instant saint," figuring he could never earn God's love
   c. attacked his carnality with brutality, thinking he had to be good to win God's love

Personal Application: Have you done these things in your life? Do you think other believers face these problems? (Please describe and comment.) _____
_____
_____

5. It is a tormenting experience for us to try to _____ through _____ what only _____ and _____ can accomplish in time.

6. It is important for us to let God mature us without our self-help efforts because:
   a. too often we try to impress others with a false sense of piety
   b. do-it-yourself righteousness and religion keeps us from being naked before God and comfortable with our own rate of growth
   c. we often struggle to produce a premature change when God-ordained change can only be accomplished in His time
   d. all the above

Personal Application: Carefully consider each answer and choose the one you personally wrestle with. What has God shown you about it? _____
_____
_____

7. It is God's will that our _____ be displayed in a cabinet of putrid, _____
    _____—openly displaying the strange dichotomy between the temporal and the eternal. It is
    amazing that God would put _____ _____ in _____ _____.
    What a glorious backdrop _____ _____ makes for His _____!

8. Many times we, like Paul, ask God to:
    a. take us away from this life
    b. look away from our willful sins so we can sin some more
    c. remove what He wants us to endure

9. The problem is that while we are changed in our spirit by the new birth, our old corruptible body and fleshly
    desires are not. They are:
    a. dominating us and everyone around us
    b. impossible to control this side of the grave
    c. spirit-controlled, but not spirit-destroyed
    d. stronger than the spirit, so we just give in

10. Despite all our washing and painting, all our grooming and exercising, this old house (the body) is still falling
    apart! Yet:
    a. we have to keep up the charade; after all, what would the neighbors think?
    b. the Holy Ghost Himself resides beneath this sagging roof
    c. we plan to move into something better someday, if we can just be "good enough"
    d. we don't know any professionals we can call to take over the project

11. The _____ _____ of us camouflage the _____ _____ in us
    with religious colloquialisms that _____ Christianity to more of an _____ than an
    _____.

12. Since the same man who wrote the majority of the New Testament said he had to keep his body "under," and
    "bring it into subjection," I:
    a. pay very little attention to those who try to impress me with the idea that they have already attained
        what is meant to be a lifelong pursuit
    b. now understand that the renewal of the old man is a daily exercise of the heart
    c. know my character is strengthened progressively day by day, not overnight
    d. all the above

Personal Application: Have you felt any of your ideas or notions "drop off" as you have read *Naked and Not
Ashamed*? If so, what has changed, and why? _____
_____
_____

13. The "bad news" is that the old house is still a _____ _____; it's still infested with
    _____. A _____ of _____ and pesky _____ crawl around in
    our heads like _____ that come out in the night.

14. Thankfully, the Guest we entertain (the Holy Spirit) desires _____ _____
    _____ than _____ _____ _____ _____!
    He enjoys neither the house nor the clothing we offer Him. He just suffers it like a _____ suffers
    adversity to be in the _____ of the one he loves.

15. Yes, we are constantly renovating through the Word of God, but the truth is:
    a.   it isn't doing any good
    b.   we could do more if we worked harder in the mission fields or on the streets of a major city
    c.   God will eventually recycle what you and I have been trying to renovate

16. The Christian life is a life of conflict, and we thank God that:
    a.   He has delivered us from it all
    b.   He (the Holy Spirit) groans and protests our sinful behavior
    c.   He gives us the freedom to turn away from conflict toward peace

Personal Application: What do you think about each of these possible answers? _____
_____
_____

17. While Saul's armor shined in the noonday sun, David fought _____, free from the entanglements of _____ _____ _____ _____. He was not _____. Even his weapon looked substandard, but his slingshot brought down the _____. We don't need the _____. We need the _____!

18. Consider the sharp contrast there is between David and King Saul, whose stately manner and pompous gait didn't stop him from being an incredible deceiver. The problem with Saul and people like him is:
    a.   they have too much money
    b.   they weren't raised right, and they were probably too pampered
    c.   they are more interested in their *image* than they are concerned about being immaculate in their hearts

19. Saul's _____ had become a breach too wide to bridge. David might have been _____, and struggled with _____ _____, but at least he was _____ _____ God!

Personal Application: If you apply the same measuring line to your own life and experiences, how do you rate on this scale? Are you more like David or Saul? _____
_____
_____

20. It is the __(select answer below)__ that must be renounced if we are to go beyond the superficial and fulfill our destiny in the supernatural.
    a.   hunger for excitement and challenge
    b.   leadership of Saul
    c.   love of nice things

21. There is a gradual and perpetual _____ _____ _____ as we walk with God. Like a chick pecking through its shell, we _____ through our concerns and over other people's _____, and break into the light to _____ _____ in a more definitive way!

Personal Application: Are you prepared to "press through" to the purposes of God for your life? Describe some specific steps you can take: _____
_____
_____
_____
_____

Chapter 9

No Additives: The Blood Alone

1. Blood is:
   a. totally irrelevant to the great spiritual truths embodied in the canonical Scriptures, particularly the wise teachings of Christ
   b. the only element in the body that reaches, affects, and fuels all other parts of the body, and illustrates the greater work of the shed blood of Jesus Christ in His Body on earth
   c. essential, for cells denied continual access to the blood can asphyxiate quickly and die as a result of internal deprivation
   d. what the physical body uses to echo and illustrate the power of the blood in the Church, the mystical Body of Christ
   e. b, c, and d

2. Apart from the blood of Christ, we do not have the _____ _____ _____ _____. Without the blood, we are only _____ sons _____ as real sons. Without His blood, we are _____-heirs trying to receive the promises _____ for the legitimate sons of God!

3. Because we have lost our teaching on the blood in this age of Pentecostalism:
   a. we have been able to relax and concentrate on true religion
   b. we have produced believers who are empowered by the Spirit but do not feel forgiven
   c. we are wasting the power of God on the problems of our past when the blood has already destroyed our past bondages
   d. b and c

4. If one of our members in the Church is unfortunate enough to fail where _____ _____ _____ _____, then we _____ them. We tie a string around them to mark them, and we _____ _____ _____ _____. We have spilled our brother's blood because his _____ is _____ from ours.

Personal Application: Can you supply an example in your own life or of someone you know who has suffered from this form of spiritual prejudice? _____
_____
_____
_____

5. Without the blood of Christ to _____ _____ and the Holy Spirit to _____ _____, no flesh can be _____. What do we mean by flesh?

_____   _____   _____

_____   _____   _____

_____   _____   _____

6. Many of our "Adams and Eves" are hiding in the bushes because (more than one may apply):
    a. that's where they belong—they are guilty and deserve every punishment God has for them
    b. we have offered no solution to the tragedies of life that afflict them
    c. we have offered no balm for the injuries that come from inner flaws and failure
    d. we have offered no *provision* for the sons and daughters who fall in sin

7. Many of us are taking the walk to _____ the _____, but we have not taken the deeper walk to _____ the fallen. When God covered Adam and Eve's nakedness, He _____ what He _____.

Personal Application: Did God do this for you? Please explain: _____
_____
_____

8. Many believers are trapped in the process of:
    a. signing up for Social Security benefits
    b. learning proper church doctrine and conduct
    c. disrobing themselves of what they have contrived in order to receive the covering God has provided
    d. properly framing and describing their eschatological views to non-believers

9. Adam stripped himself before a holy God, admitted his tragic sins, and still _____
_____ _____ as a son in the presence of God. Adam and Eve realized in that moment that:
    a. they had been caught, and they needed to go along with God until they could psychoanalyze away their guilt in a private place
    b. the only solution for their sin was in the perfect provision of their loving God
    c. the only way they could "live on" was to be "wrapped in the coverings of the lamb's life"
    d. had it not been for the blood, neither of them would have been there
    e. b, c, and d

10. All creation is waiting for the sons of God to "come to themselves" and:
    a. love like Jesus loves
    b. become what we were meant to be in terms of honesty and transparency
    c. completely disrobe and dislodge ourselves from the many-layered clothes of vain religiosity
    d. all the above

11. It is important to be as open about our failures as we are about our successes because (choose all that apply):
    a. that's what good religious folks do—they talk a lot
    b. without that kind of honesty, we create a false image that causes others to needlessly struggle
    c. when others hear our one-sided testimony of successes with *no failure*, they become discouraged
    d. they think that they are "wrestling" and struggling while we seem to "have it together"

12. You are blessed if:
    a. your bank account, new car, and up-to-date clothing fashion show it
    b. you receive everything you ask God to give you, right when you want it
    c. you find someone who can see your flaws and your underdeveloped character, *and love you in spite of it all*

Personal Application: Please give examples to illustrate or prove the validity of your answer: _____
_____
_____
_____
_____

13. It is the _____ of God that leads to _____. Repentance doesn't come because of the _____ _____ and _____ of raging ministers who need mercy them- selves. Repentance comes because of the _____ _____ of a perfect God, a God who cares for the _____ _____ that others would have _____.

14. "Accepting the rejected" is:
    a. the whining motto of do-gooders who are soft on hardened criminals and perverts
    b. not the weakness of the gospel, but its strength
    c. the motivation for us to extend soft hands and tender words to the distraught heart that seeks so desper- ately for a place of refuge
    d. b and c

15. When we hold out our arms to the halt and the lame, the deaf and the dumb, to come to Christ the cure, we know:
    a. they will need much of the Word and much time before their marriages cease to tremble and their self-images improve
    b. they will have flashbacks and relapses, and require intensive care
    c. that most of our "doctors" have at one time or another been patients, and that many are still being treated
    d. all the above

Personal Application: Which of these answers do you identify with the most? Please explain: _____
_____
_____
_____
_____

16. While we box ourselves in and lift ourselves up as the "epitome of sanctity":
    a. we really don't need anything else; we're a finished product in Christ, needing only "maintenance doses" of the Word on Sunday mornings
    b. beneath our stained glass windows and padded pews lay broken hearts and torn families
    c. we have no right to be blessed, in ourselves; we are neither worthy nor deserving of it—He has blessed us "in spite of ourselves"
    d. b and c

17. When Jesus was on the cross, He was still preaching as they watched Him dying—_____ and _____ _____! Even though you may have been _____ and oth- ers have beheld your nakedness, there are still some who will _____ _____ _____. Some dying thief will relate to you—if you can, like Jesus, _____ through your _____ and _____ through your _____.

18. We, as the Body of Christ, may be hiding beneath a "loincloth" that has stifled our testimony and blocked our ability to be transparent if:
    a. we prefer Western-style art depicting the crucifixion
    b. we follow some unspoken order whereby we are not allowed to share our struggles as well as our successes
    c. we feel obligated to maintain some false image of perfection in order to be serviceable to our society
    d. the loincloth represents all those things that are *humanly imposed upon us*—things that God does not require
    e. b, c, and d

19. By hiding our humanity beneath the man-made cloths of religiosity, we have _____ _____ what God has _____ _____!

20. We should apologize for ever trying to pass ourselves off as anything more than men made of clay who have the power of God (more than one may apply):
    a. because we need no loincloth; the Body of Christ was meant to be naked and not ashamed
    b. because like the physical body of Christ, we have been camouflaged beneath religious loincloths
    c. because like Adam's fig leaves, our loincloth is our attempt to cover what only God can cover
    d. but if we do, people will see how flawed we are and they won't listen to us anymore

21. The body of Christ was meant to be covered with nothing but the blood of Christ. This means (choose all that apply):
    a. all the painters who painted loincloths were pagans and doomed to hell
    b. God's provision for our nudity was the blood of Jesus Christ
    c. He knew that the death angel would soon pass by, and loincloths do not impress him
    d. when we go on trial, we have only one defense: We must plead, *"No additives; the blood alone!"*

Chapter 10

He Laid Aside His Garments

1. For those of us who have had a "reality check" through the unveiling of Judas, supper is over because (choose all that apply):
    a. we now realize that our ultimate purpose for gathering isn't really for fellowship
    b. it's not so fun anymore, and we need to get out of the whole thing
    c. He really gathered us to sharpen and prune us through our attempts at fellowship
    d. the people we worship with are the "utensils" the Lord uses to perfect us

2. It is only a matter of time before we realize that all the guests around the table of the Lord (choose all that apply):
    a. are merely patients (like we are)—just mutilated, torn, dilapidated, disfigured caricatures of social grace and ambiance
    b. are bleeding
    c. have some sort of gross deformity beneath their gracious smiles
    d. are better than we are, and we wonder why we are even trying to pretend we belong

Personal Application: When you read these answers, are you offended or relieved? Why? Explain: _____
_____
_____
_____
_____
_____
_____
_____

3. The Lord Jesus told us in Luke 14 to go out quickly into the streets and bring in the "_____, and the _____, and the _____, and the _____." To do this, we must make the transition every believer must make: the transition _____ _____ to _____ time.

4. If you leave the fellowship around His table after taking a closer look at the membership, you will discover (choose all that apply):
    a. that you were right; nobody is quite up to your standards
    b. that somewhere a perfect church is waiting for your appearance to round out its collection of the elect
    c. the sad fact that every ministry, regardless of its size or structure, has its own incapacities
    d. it is time for you to learn the art of service and move beyond the gluttony of supper

5. If supper has ended in your life (choose all that apply):
    a. you may want to stay where you are, but you have to go where He calls
    b. you will have to wait until the dinner bell rings again
    c. you may want to desperately go back to your original naiveté (but you can't)
    d. you will know it when you are being betrayed by those you trust

6. Once supper is ended, there is no need for you to hold on to your plate and spoon. God gave you a
_____ of _____ in a time of need to accomplish what was necessary, but:
   a. you may be tempted to stay at the supper table to "get all you can, and 'can' all you get"
   b. you may want to never rise from the table, and rest on the laurels of indifference and contentment instead
   c. He wants you to rise from the cluttered table and heed the need to move on
   d. all the above

7. We have lingered around the cluttered table, and (choose all that apply):
   a. we have chattered away the age and jested away a generation
   b. now that we have eaten so well, we need a nice rest and a gentle time to fold our hands and reflect on the bounty of the Lord
   c. we are sitting around the cluttered dishes of dead programs whose crushed crumbs are not enough to feed our impoverished generation
   d. we need men and women who will rise from supper because even the waiter has gone home, and we sit in the same spot rehearsing the same excuses

Personal Application: When you selected your answers, who did you picture in your mind? Was it yourself, or somebody else? Please explain: _____
_____
_____
_____
_____

8. Your comfort zone is destroyed when:
   a. you are forced to eat and fellowship with your friends, family, and other people who are just like you
   b. you must go through the unnerving process of disrobing in a room where all others are clothed, making you feel like you are the only one who is naked
   c. your fear of "being different" closes you in a prison of disobedience because you are afraid of being alone
   d. b and c

9. Jesus paid the price and _____ _____ His _____ before those whom He had labored to _____. Unfortunately, we have not followed His example as leaders or sheep. We have asked our leaders to be more than what _____ _____ _____ _____, and we have imprisoned them in their _____ and chained them to their _____.

10. The _____ _____ _____ will never be unleashed until those who are called to deliver it find the grace, or perhaps the mercy, that will allow them to:
   a. finally be recognized for who they are, and to flow in their gifts as they rightly deserve
   b. complete another course of study to earn their ministerial degree and enter the ministry with full credentials and preparation
   c. rise above their fellows and above the wounded sheep as a shining beacon of deeper devotion and richer resources than those they oversee
   d. lay aside their garments, as Jesus Himself stooped to bless the men whom He had taught

11. Peter said, "Lord, not my feet only, but also my hands and my head" (Jn. 13:9). Yet we're still _____ and fuming over exposing, _____, and _____ one another's feet! We have never _____ people in the Church. We have never allowed people—_____ _____—to find a _____ at our table!

12. Ministry is birthed when you are stripped down to your heart's desire, and something in your heart says more than anything else (choose all that apply):
    a. "I'm really good at talking and counseling. I think I would make a good pastor—if the money's good."
    b. "I can do a better job than all the people I see filling the pulpits. It's time for me to start my own thing *and do it right for a change!*"
    c. "I want my life to count for something. I want to accomplish something for God."
    d. "Oh God, don't let me impress anyone else but the One to whom I gave my life."

Personal Application: Compare the answers you chose with those you rejected. Which answers echo the heart of God, and why? _____

_____

_____

_____

13. The "garment" represents different things to different people, such as (choose all that apply):
    a. whatever camouflages our realness
    b. whatever hinders us from really affecting our environment
    c. the personal agendas we have set for ourselves (many of which God was never consulted about)
    d. the "fig coverings" we have contrived for ourselves to hide our embarrassments

Personal Application: Which of these best describes *your garment*? Explain: _____

_____

_____

_____

14. Every person who finds real purpose will, sooner or later:
    a. write a book about it
    b. learn how to avoid every trial and difficulty by using God's Word
    c. go through the fire and give it all up
    d. go through some series of adversities that will cause them to let go of the temporal and cleave to the eternal

15. True worship is born when _____ _____ occurs. You can never be really _____ until you personally experience a situation that calls you to _____ _____ your _____. It is _____ you _____ _____ and _____ _____ that seasons you into the real aroma of worship.

16. Jesus showed His disciples that they could never change the atmosphere or wash the feet of anybody until they had gone through sacrifice and endured risk and rejection. Laying aside your garments requires you to say (choose all that apply):
    a. "Here are my grudges and unforgiveness"
    b. "Here is my need to impress and be acknowledged"
    c. "Here is my time and my overtime"
    d. "Here is my second job, and anything I may be wrapped up in that hinders me from receiving new glory"
    e. none of the above

17. At the "final supper," Jesus laid aside His garments; in the garden, He laid aside His will! In our century, great evangelists and ministers have touched the world because (more than one may apply):
    a. they knew how to use the media
    b. the things they laid aside made them who they were
    c. they had everything going for them
    d. they did what God is calling *you* to do: lay aside your garments and serve

18. There are no differences in the feet of _____ _____ and the feet of the one who _____ them. Your ministry becomes truly effective when you know that there is precious little _____ between the _____ _____ _____ and yourself.

19. Although Jesus normally dressed with distinction, in the upper room He did His real ministry with a complete _____ of distinction by:
    a. making a lasting impact on His disciples with His forceful words
    b. making a lasting impact on His disciples by disrobing, covering Himself only with a serving towel, and humbly washing their feet
    c. losing the respect of His disciples
    d. telling the disciples they were going to have to take over the ministry when He left so they could now begin campaigning and voting for the Number One position

20. The final touch of God was delivered through a Man who had humbled Himself and:
    a. wrapped His vulnerabilities up and hid them (True/False)
    b. He was covered like a servant, ready to help the hurting (True/False)
    c. His suit, His clerical attire, consisted mostly of an expensive, seamless robe (True/False)
    d. His ministry was best seen when He wrapped Himself in a towel, not when He debated in the temple (True/False)

21. Don't join the spiritual elitists who are impressed with their own speech if (choose all that apply):
    a. you believe that God will exalt you in due season
    b. you believe you have the ability to wash the dusty sands of life from the feet of this world
    c. you are willing to lay aside every distraction and garment
    d. you long to wrap every naked human flaw in the warm towel of servanthood as you help others and draw the water

Personal Application: Which of these answers touch your soul? What will you do in response? _____
_____
_____

Chapter 11

Stripped for Prayer

1. While others sleep, some of us:
    a. walk the floor at night as a mother with a suckling child
    b. have a conversation where there are no ears to hear
    c. find no solace in ordinary things in the middle of the night
    d. have a restlessness, almost an anticipation, that something is about to happen
    e. all the above

2. In the stillness of the night, as divinely inspired and disturbed sleepwalkers, we often look at something
    _____ _____. We speak the _____ to the _____, birthing a
    prayer...a feeble cry of a heart whose _____ has pushed the head to bow in humble
    _____ to One greater than itself.

3. "Real prayer" is:
    a. reserved for real problems that cannot be easily prayed through in public
    b. not made for human ears
    c. easily heard in every public church meeting across the globe
    d. a nausea of the mind, bringing up the unresolved past that swirls around and around in us

Personal Application: Have you ever experienced "real prayer"? Describe what happened: _____
_____
_____
_____

4. If we can relieve the brokenness in our hearts only through unhindered groanings before the throne of God,
    then (choose all that apply, then explain your choices):
    a. religion and its images can do much to effectively relieve our brokenheartedness
    b. there is nothing more involved here than the mere pious sputterings of religious refinement
    c. it is a midnight cry for divine assistance!
    d. what we convey around others is more like a plastic-covered superficial replica of what real prayer is
        all about; it is a dressed up, Sunday-go-to-meeting counterfeit that is impressive but inconsequential
_____
_____
_____

5. Our jet-set, microwave age has produced some elaborate and intricately designed places of worship, complete
    with (choose all that apply):
    a. the liturgical order of pious hearts whose heads have contrived a method that seems spiritually edifying
    b. highly anointed and properly motivated worship and ministry
    c. a remarkable emphasis on facilities marked by impressive sanctuaries, stately auditoriums, and distin-
        guished people who rush in to fill them for a punctual hour of spiritual rhetoric
    d. well-orchestrated services complete with pomp and circumstance

6. Bishop T.D. Jakes said his purpose was "to point out the inconsistency that blares in [his] heart like a trumpet." He said he:
   a. was distracted by the bleating of the sheep, who bleed behind the stained glass and upon the padded pew
   b. blames all our success for their pain
   c. proposes that if we eliminate the ornateness, we would cure the ills of our society
   d. couldn't help but wonder if we have majored on the minor and consequently minored on the major

7. Nothing fuels prayer like:
   a. the right background music
   b. a good night's sleep, a proper diet, and a wholesome attitude
   c. need
   d. a good and proper religious upbringing

Personal Application: Please describe a personal prayer experience that illustrates the answer you selected: ___
_____
_____

8. We live among men who (choose all that apply):
   a. are innately good, wise, and capable of running the affairs of families and nations with great skill
   b. have replaced creations for the Creator
   c. have brilliant minds that grasp facts, but fail to perceive truth
   d. until they come to truth, will escape the thing that humbles the heart and bends the will to the posture of prayer

9. Each of us must have the _____ and the _____ _____ to move beyond our images into our realities. It is difficult, sometimes even painful, to face the truth about our _____ and then possess the courage to ask for _____ _____ for our lives.

10. "Wrapped in the sanctity of _____ _____ _____, we often hide the nudity of _____ _____ _____. We can easily find ourselves _____ much more than we _____ _____. Nothing _____ us as effectively as a trial, though.

11. People miss wonderful opportunities for God's blessing because:
    a. they have "an image to uphold"
    b. they lack the humility to assume a posture of receiving and accept God's gift through other men
    c. their spiritual arrogance will not allow them to open their hearts to the flawed vessels God uses
    d. all the above

Personal Application: Have you seen any of these during your life? Explain: _____
_____
_____

12. Satan makes his attack when you are hungry (hunger is a _____ _____). The extreme test of faith is to stand fast when you have a _____ _____ you could satisfy in an _____ way.

13. There are some people who have not been released from old trials yet because:
    a. they haven't been good enough
    b. they will not allow God to heal them through the angels of ministry He has chosen to use
    c. they have been through so much that they simply don't trust anymore; needing *someone*, they don't trust *anyone*
    d. unlike Jesus, they refused to let someone they considered their "lesser" to minister to them

14. If the winds of adversity beat fiercely enough and if the rains plummet down with enough thunderous force, then we are _____ by the _____ and brought to a place of _____, _____ prayer.

Personal Application: Have you ever been brought to this place? Please describe it: _____
_____
_____

15. The place of _____ prayer is illustrated by _____ in First Samuel chapter 1. This kind of prayer is effective because (choose all that apply):
    a. it is offered up by people who have gotten to the point where they lost their self-consciousness because they got sick and tired of allowing the enemy subdue what God has given them
    b. it comes from hearts whose only prayer is: "All I want is to get well"
    c. it is propelled by a power that boggles the mind, a power from somewhere below our image and our name, even beyond the opinions of others
    d. like Hannah, we may find that with so much locked up in us, when we begin to empty ourselves out, we may appear to be drunk or beside ourselves—even to the leadership of the church

16. The radical Christians coming to the forefront today (choose all that apply):
    a. are so unconventional that they're not even saved
    b. have nothing to lose
    c. like Christ, they have been stripped on the cross and are speaking the truth—even under the threat of nails and spears
    d. pray, "I have been stripped! I have learned the power of transparency and the strength of being backed into a corner"
    e. all the above

Personal Application: Which of these answers should apply to you? Why? Explain: _____
_____
_____

17. We "learn faith" when our options diminish because faith is reserved for those times when _____
_____ _____ _____, when "push" has collided with "shove"! Faith comes alive when there is nothing we can do but be _____ by the _____—or look unto the Invisible to do the _____!

18. Faith must have the _____ of _____ to exhibit its illustrious ability. After all (more than one many apply):
    a. it is just a test with a reward
    b. the greater the conflict is, the more likely you won't come through it in one piece
    c. there is a certain tightness needed to cause faith to be secreted (you can't even get toothpaste out of a tube without a firm squeeze)
    d. there is something good in you, and God knows how to get it out

19. The pressure is mounting. Let us:
    a. get out of town while we still can
    b. discard what we don't need so we can activate what we do need
    c. lay aside every sin that would so easily beset us, and forgive everyone who ever hurt us or disappointed us
    d. stop deliberating over the acts of men and prepare to see an act of God

Personal Application: Do any of the answers you selected trigger a painful response? Explain: _____
_____
_____

20. As part of a radical response to God's radical call, you may have to walk the floor, or (choose all that apply):
    a. confess some issues that you may not want to confront—which is *naked prayer*
    b. forgive someone who didn't even ask to be forgiven (do it anyway)
    c. let the cool waters of God's Word rinse the residue from your past
    d. spread every issue in your heart before God (He can't cleanse what you will not expose)
    e. bathe your mind in the streams of His mercy

Personal Application: Make these answers a "Checklist for Healing." One by one, honestly ask yourself if you have done these things. If you haven't, do them, and be healed in His grace.

21. This kind of renewal can only occur in the heart of someone who has been *through enough* to (choose all that apply):
    a. open his heart
    b. close up his past
    c. stand in the rain of God's grace
    d. tell the next generation the truth: "The only way you can dress up for God is to lay before Him as a naked offering, a living sacrifice offered up at the altar in *naked prayer*!"

Personal Application: Again, go through this list and make sure you fully qualify for the fulfillment of God's renewal process in your life!

Answer Key

Chapter 1: The Fear of the Father

1. strong, heart, weaken
2. lethal; d; personalized response
3. c, d
4. a to f (as applicable); personalized response
5. hidden part, child in us; c,d, or e as applicable, plus additional personal comments
6. a to c as applicable, with personalized response
7. b; personalized response
8. a to d as applicable; personalized response
9. a to d as applicable
10. a to d as applicable, with small group discussion
11. c
12. c
13. identity, son, daughter; a to c as applicable, with discussion
14. fear, depart, terror, healthy attitude, respect
15. secure, relationship, love
16. approve, loves
17. conviction, condemnation
18. conviction
19. d

Chapter 2: No Secrets in the Secret Place

1. awaken, God, sleeps, slumbers
2. b
3. d
4. under the bushes, transparent
5. conspire, deceive; personal application
6. properly draped, wrapped, own identity

7. a. enjoy, relationship
    b. sit, lap
    c. accepted
    d. scars, bruised hearts
    personalized response

8. a to c as applicable; personalized response

9. silence, secrecy, ridiculous; personal answers may vary, but essentially it is because He already sees what we're trying to hide, He already hears what we're trying to silence, and He already perceives the thoughts we're trying to bury

10. condemn us, esteems, redeems

11. develop arrogance, frightened, emotional dysfunction

12. personalized response

13. open-hearted communication; c, d

14. on the operating table, surgeon; personalized response

15. c

16. a to d, with small group discussion

17. cleansing grace, clean, purify, hide, secret corners

18. cleansed at Calvary, renewed, day to day; personalized response

19. a to d as applicable

20. worship, correctly, wrestling, unconfessed

21. drop the towel, stand naked, trust, hope

Chapter 3: Superman Is Dead

1. d

2. c

3. great courage, limitations, sufficiency; personalized response

4. a. personalized response
    b. personalized response
    c. Someone going through your two responses in letter a or who is fighting a losing battle with your response in letter b.

5. "Take an ordinary man from an ordinary background, saddle him with responsibility and tremendous visibility, and tell him, 'You must be god-like.' "

6. eat a perfect word, stained hands

7. lowly, heroes, not perfect, powerful; personalized response

8. a. "someone who puts himself at risk to help someone else"
    b. Jesus Christ
    c. personalized response

9. didn't let the stink, saving the man

10. a. jealousy, cruelty
    b. ostracized
    c. criticized
    d. serve, blows, satan
    e. stabs
    f. minister

11. strong sense, destiny; personalized response

12. survive, save anyone

13. d

14. convinced, promised, able to perform, people, move, direction; personalized response

15. c, with personal comments on each answer

16. army, rejects, experience rejection; personalized response

17. d

18. place, misplaced; personalized response

19. recycling, lives; d

20. d

Chapter 4: The Power of Passion

1. ecstasy, pain, crisis, cross, purpose, cross

2. e

3. reality, fulfillment, no passion, uncomfortable

4. personal passion, achieve, wall; personalized response

5. d

6. Suffering, passion, desire

7. c, d; personalized response

8. c

9. b, c, d; personalized response

10. d

11. what, endure, deeply, desire; personalized response

12. c

13. exemplified, coming, consummated, His dying

14. is no power; e

15. a, c, d

16. strength, passion, heart, heart, issues, life

17. d

18. focus, protected; c; personalized response

19. verge, miracles, perpetual, vulnerability; personalized response

20. treasure, surrounded, trash; personalized response

21. d

22. present desire, passion, continue, naked, ashamed

Chapter 5: Reaping the Rewards of Your Own Thoughts

1. work, no good, eternal Companion, best

2. embers, counsel, thoughts, how to be alone

3. stressless, anxieties, concerns, youthful; personalized response

4. relax, enjoy life, fire, own thoughts

5. a to c as applicable, with small group discussion

6. in the past, happened yesterday, endured, survived, not what happened

7. remote control; d

8. move in, rearrange furniture, goals, dreams, ambitions

9. c

10. private battleground; a to d as applicable

11. a and f, b and d, c and e; personalized response

12. placenta; b

13. c, d; c and d are true because they have caused countless numbers of individuals to rise above the problems in choices a and b

14. d

15. excommunicating, thoughts, buried, rubble, minds; personalized response

16. c

17. turn away, nagging memories, symphonies, enlightenment

18. thought, action, power, words, positively; d

19. c, d

20. a to d as applicable; personalized response

21. field, dreams, water your own field

Chapter 6: The Cold Kiss of a Calloused Heart

1. c

2. jealousy, time, commitment, quality, quantity

3. d

4. d; personalized response

5. e; personalized response

6. b, c, d; personalized response

7. a to e as applicable; personalized response

8. direction, rejection, Judas', God, wise, aborted, paranoia, restrict, exploring, friendships, relationships

9. relationship, flourish; personalized response

10. closes doors; d

11. negative, painful betrayals; c; personalized response

12. uses, negative, positive, sovereignty

13. c; personalized response

14. injuries, adversity; c

15. c

16. instrumental, embraced, affirmed, Judas sector; personalized response

17. d

18. actions, purpose, God, friend, malice, strife, catalyst, greatness

19. painful, negative; b, c, d

20. c, d (b is optional); personalized response

21. accompanied by survival

Chapter 7: Survive the Crash of Relationships

1. sense purpose, creative, accept events

2. b, c, d (a is optional)

3. strip, dependent, self-reliance, God-reliance

4. physical pain, healing, restoration

5. c (a and b also have some truth)

6. resolved issues, keep, pain; c

7. e; personalized response

8. e

9. e; personalized response

10. c

11. b, c, d

12. c

13. God's selection, people's rejection; personalized response

14. everything; d

15. orchestrates, accomplish, purpose, painful circumstances; personalized response

16. c

17. remove, endure, immovable, worst things

18. d

19. c; personalized response

20. bless you, disregard, mess, cannot lie, bruises

21. d; personalized response

Chapter 8: Help! My New Heart Is Living in an Old Body!

 1. outer relationships, inward revelation, on Christ

 2. f

 3. d
   a. loves
   b. doesn't
   c. roller coaster

 4. c; personalized response

 5. accomplish, ourselves, God, maturity

 6. d; personalized response

 7. treasure, unregenerated flesh, so much, so little, our weakness, strength

 8. c

 9. c

10. b

11. very best, very worst, reduce, act, attitude

12. d; personalized response

13. death trap, rodents, legion, thoughts, memories, roaches

14. more for us, we have in us, lover, company

15. c

16. b; personalized response

17. naked, trying to be impressive, ashamed, giant, superficial, supernatural

18. c

19. deceitfulness, weak, moral issues, naked before; personalized response

20. b

21. transference of authority, press, opinions, know God; personalized response

Chapter 9: No Additives: The Blood Alone

 1. e

 2. proof of our sonship, bastard, camouflaged, pseudo, reserved

 3. d

 4. we are very strong, condemn, deny them the blood, sin, different; personalized response

 5. save it, empower it, saved; personalized response (virtually no answer referring to living people can be wrong)

 6. b, c, d

7. discover, fallen, cover, covered, discovered; personalized response

8. c

9. maintained his position; e

10. d

11. b, c, d

12. c; personalized response (it should mention God, since He loved us "while we were yet sinners")

13. goodness, repentance, scare tactics, threats, unfailing love, cracked vases, discarded

14. d

15. d; personalized response

16. d

17. naked, not ashamed, stripped, hear your words, preach, nudity, minister, pain

18. e

19. covered up, made bare

20. a, b, c

21. b, c, d

Chapter 10: He Laid Aside His Garments

1. a, c, d

2. a, b, c; personalized response

3. poor, maimed, halt, blind, from suppertime, service

4. c, d

5. a, c, d

6. period, innocence; d

7. a, c, d; personalized response

8. d

9. laid aside, garments, inspire, we could ever be, callings, giftings

10. power of ministry; d

11. squirming, forgiving, washing, accepted, real people, place

12. c, d; personalized response (answers a and b are rooted in wrong motives and attitudes)

13. a, b, c, d; personalized response

14. d

15. true sacrifice, anointed, lay aside, garments, what, left behind, laid aside

16. a, b, c, d

17. b, d

18. the washed, washes, difference, people you serve

19. loss; b

20. a. False
    b. True
    c. False
    d. True

21. a, b, c, d; personalized response

Chapter 11: Stripped for Prayer

1. e

2. beyond vision, inaudible, Intangible, conflict, submission

3. a, b, d; personalized response

4. c, d; personalized response

5. a, c, d

6. a, d

7. c; personalized response

8. b, c, d

9. curiosity, inner thirst, circumstances, God's best

10. what we profess, what we possess, professing, honestly possess, disrobes

11. d; personalized response

12. legitimate need, legitimate need, illegitimate

13. b, c, d

14. stripped, struggle, open, naked; personalized response

15. naked, Hannah; a, b, c, d

16. b, c, d; personalized response

17. there are no options, crushed, inevitable, impossible

18. incubator, impossibility; b, c, d

19. b, c, d; personalized response

20. a, b, c, d, e (all are vital points of victory)

21. a, b, c, d (together these comprise a wholesome description of God-ordained health, wholeness, and healing for the man and woman of God who can stand naked and not ashamed!)

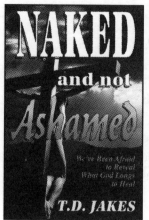

JAKES
T.D.
Workbooks

WOMAN, THOU ART LOOSED! WORKBOOK
by Bishop T.D. Jakes.

Whether studying in a group or as an individual, this workbook will help you learn and apply the truths found in *Woman, Thou Art Loosed!* If you're searching to increase your spiritual growth, then this workbook is for you.

TPB-48p.
ISBN 1-56043-810-X
(8½" X 11") Retail $6.99

CAN YOU STAND TO BE BLESSED? WORKBOOK
by Bishop T.D. Jakes.

Are you ready to unlock the inner strength to go on in God? This workbook will help you apply the book's principles to your life. Appropriate for individual or small group study.

TPB-48p.
ISBN 1-56043-812-6
(8½" X 11") Retail $6.99

Available at your local Christian bookstore
or by calling toll free:
Destiny Image
1-800-722-6774
Visit us on the Internet:
http://www.reapernet.com

T.D. JAKES

Videos

DESERT BABIES
by T.D. Jakes.

Like the generation of Israelites born in the wilderness, we too are destined to *possess the promised land.* Yet we also need to learn the lesson their childhood of changes and challenges taught them—to stay ready to move with God! In this message T.D. Jakes shares what God can do in and through the life of a survivor as he or she gets ready for His next move.
1 Video
ISBN 1-56043-389-2
Retail $29.99

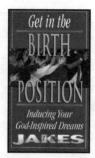

GET IN THE BIRTH POSITION
by T.D. Jakes.

God's Word is steadfast. Nothing can stop what God has promised from coming to pass. However, you need to get ready. In this message T.D. Jakes shares the steps necessary to bring to birth the promises of God in your life.
1 Video
ISBN 1-56043-397-3
Retail $29.99

HE LOVED ME ENOUGH TO BE LATE
by T.D. Jakes.

Many of us have wondered, "God, what is taking You so long?" Often God doesn't do what we think He will, when we think He will, because He loves us. His love is willing to be criticized to accomplish its purpose. Jesus chose to wait until Lazarus had been dead four days, and still raised him up! This message will challenge you to roll away your doubt and receive your miracle from the tomb!
1 Video
ISBN 1-56043-396-5
Retail $29.99

MANPOWER
by T.D. Jakes.

Wounded men will experience the transforming power of God's Word in *Manpower.* Satan has plotted to destroy the male, but God will raise up literally thousands of men through this life-changing, soul-cleansing, and mind-renewing word. This 4-part video series is for every man who ever had an issue he could not discuss; and for every man who needed to bare his heart and had no one to hear it.
4 Videos
ISBN 1-56043-394-9
Retail $99.99

THE 25TH HOUR
by T.D. Jakes.

Have you ever thought, "Lord, I need more time"? Joshua thought the same thing, and he called upon the sun and moon to stand still! This message from Joshua 10 testifies of the mightiness of our God, who can stop time and allow His children to accomplish His purposes and realize the victory!
1 Video
ISBN 1-56043-399-X
Retail $29.99

**Available at your local Christian bookstore
or by calling Destiny Image toll free: 1-800-722-6774
Visit us on the Internet: http://www.reapernet.com**

1996
WHAT TO DO
WHEN YOU DON'T KNOW WHAT TO DO

The Adventure Journal is your day-by-day Bible study resource. It contains instructions for the eight Adventure themes, five Action Steps, daily Scripture readings and assignments, and provides journaling space each day. Journals are available in age-graded versions for adults, teens, children in grades 3-6, and children from kindergarten to grade 2.

The Adventure guidebook *When Life Becomes a Maze* is a practical aid to completing the 50-Day Adventure. It will give you a biblical perspective for trusting Christ in times of confusion, motivate you to negotiate the mazes of life, and suggest numerous practical ways to implement the 50-Day Adventure themes and Action Steps into your spiritual walk.

Adult Journal	1-879050-70-6	$6.00
Student Journal	1-879050-71-4	$6.00
Children's Journal (3-6)	1-879050-73-0	$6.00
Children's Activity Book (K-2)	1-879050-74-9	$6.00
Children's Scripture Memory Tape	1-879050-81-1	$6.00
When Life Becomes a Maze	1-879050-77-3	$6.00
When Life Becomes a Maze audiobook	1-879050-79-X	$12.00
"Believe It or Not" Scripture Promise Pack	1-879050-82-X	$1.00
Spanish Adult Journal	1-879050-83-8	$6.00
Braille Adult Journal	1-56043-706-5	$12.00
Point-of-Purchase Adventure Materials Display	1-56043-730-8	$30.00

Available at your local Christian bookstore

or by calling toll free:

Destiny Image

1-800-722-6774

Visit us on the Internet:

http://www.reapernet.com

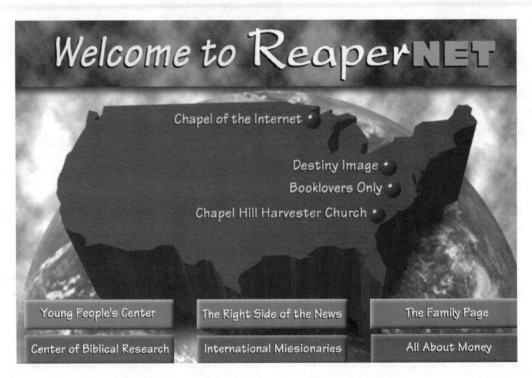